NLP for Tweens

Judy Bartkowiak

Paperback ISBN 9781780922508
ePub ISBN 9781780922515
PDF ISBN 9781780922522

Published in the UK by MX Publishing
335 Princess Park Manor, Royal Drive, London, N11 3GX
www.mxpublishing.co.uk

Cover design by www.staunch.com

MEET JUDY

You do not need to know anything about NLP to enjoy this book; in fact it probably helps if you've never heard of it before because I will explain everything as we go along.

This book is yours; write notes in it, underline things, answer the questions and generally get involved with it! Some parts will be relevant now and others may be more useful in a year or two as it's for children aged about 10-13yrs.

It starts with a 'getting to know yourself' chapter with quizzes. Then we move on to some basics of NLP to show you how to use it for the situations you will experience during these tween years.

Then there are some specific chapters on confidence, motivation and goal setting, emotional ups and downs, body matters and relationships. These are full of questions and exercises for you to complete and learn from. Find out how to feel better about yourself, learn from your mistakes and get the results you want, both in school and out of school.

I am qualified and experienced in neuro linguistic programming (NLP) which is a collection of tools and techniques that companies have been using for years. They use NLP for leadership, sales and management training but I've adapted it to suit your age group and the sort of situations you will encounter.

As well as helping children and teenagers with problems, I am a writer of NLP and Children's books. You can buy them from my Bookshop

I live in Burnham, Buckinghamshire with my husband Edward and our four children aged 11-24yrs, a dog and loads of chickens.

ENGAGING NLP

Did you know that every day around us there are millions of things to see and hear and loads of feelings we could have about them.

BUT

at any point in time we only notice 9 of them.
The funny thing is that each of us notices a different 9 things and that is what makes us unique.
What we pay attention to makes us different.
What we say and how we say it makes us different.
What we do and how we do it makes us different
Every day we make choices about what we notice, what we say and what we do.
Sometimes these choices make us happy and sometimes they make us sad.
I want you to learn about how using NLP can help you make choices that make you happy.

CONTENTS

Page

CHAPTER 1: WHO DO YOU THINK YOU ARE?

This chapter is full of short quizzes which will help you get to know yourself better. What you find out here will help you to understand why you get on well with some people and not others and how you engage in some lessons but not others. Once you know this, you can apply it to how you make friends and how you learn best, making you more popular and giving you better grades.

Have you heard of Visual, Auditory, and Kinaesthetic? Do you know which you are already? Basically you are visual if you tend to notice what you see, auditory if you focus on what you hear and kinaesthetic when you focus on what you do or feel. Although you use all three at different times, there will be one that you prefer and feel most comfortable with. Here is a quiz to help you work out whether you are visual, auditory or kinaesthetic.

Q1. You're watching a movie with some friends, what do you notice most?

    a) What the characters look like and what they are wearing
    b) The music, sound track and the voices
    c) What they are doing, the action

Q2. When you think about what you'll be doing next weekend, you

    a) Can picture yourself doing it
    b) Want to chat about it with your friends
    c) You feel excited already

Q3. When you have an argument with your parents you …

    a) Look angry and take an aggressive stance
    b) Shout a lot
    c) Can be quite physical

Q4. After a holiday you like to ….

    a) Look at the photos
    b) Chat about it
    c) Remember what fun it was and what you did

Q5. You're off to a friend's sleepover, do you think about

    a) What you will wear
    b) What you will talk about
    c) What you will do

Q6. On your mobile phone you spend more time

    a) Texting and looking at your photos
    b) Calling your friends
    c) Playing with the apps

Q7. Your favourite subjects at school are

    a) Anything arty
    b) Anything musical
    c) Anything physical like sport or dancing

Q8. When you're feeling ill what concerns you most is

    a) What you look like
    b) What you sound like
    c) What you feel like

Q9. Thinking about your best mate…

    a) You look quite similar
    b) You talk about the same things
    c) You like to do similar things

Q10. You want a job one day that will be

    a) Arty or creative in some way
    b) Connected with music
    c) Physical

Number of As   ☐

Number of Bs   ☑

Number of Cs   ☐

A - Visual

If you answered mostly 'A' then you are more visual. You think in pictures and images. You will remember what you've seen and will be observant. You notice body language and facial expressions and can know a lot about people before they've even spoken. Visual people tend to speak quite quickly. Do your friends tell you to 'slow down!'? Your descriptions will be colourful and bright and your surroundings will be important to you as will your appearance.

You will (if you're allowed) have pictures and photos all over the wall of your bedroom and you will have wanted to help choose the colour scheme. Your clothes will be important to you and you enjoy shopping for new clothes that capture the look you're after. You'll enjoy flicking through magazines for ideas about fashion and notice what the celebs are wearing. You'll probably watch programmes on TV about fashion and makeover. You'll spend ages getting ready to go out as you need to look perfect. You'll certainly notice what your friends are wearing and be embarrassed if they look bad because you won't want to be seen with them.

Boys, you too can be visual and you care how you look. Your emphasis may be on your body and muscles, building up that 'six pack' and impressing the girls with your physique and hair. You want to look your best and follow fashion, wearing the top brands. You can't wait to drive and what your first car looks like will be more important than what is under the bonnet. Colour, lines and style will be considered and discussed with friends for hours.

If you are visual then you will learn best from seeing rather than hearing, so make notes in class because you'll remember what you see in your notes much better than trying to remember what was said. You will find mind maps, flash cards and visual representations of facts helpful when you're revising because it will stay in your head better like that. Tony Buzan has written lots of excellent books and has produced software that you can use to make your own mind maps. Use YouTube videos and BBC I player, DVDs and whatever else you can find that appeals to your visual senses.

When you're trying to remember something look up to your left because that's where the images are stored in your brain. If you're trying to imagine something you haven't seen before then look up to your right to find it.

B - Auditory

If you answered more B then you are auditory and probably love music, notice the sounds around you and prefer your friends to call rather than text or email. You tend to remember what people say to you or what you've heard better than what you've read. You might use expressions like 'Listen up' or 'shut up'.

An auditory person usually makes and enjoys a lot of noise and sounds are important to them. They will like singing, musical instruments and noisy video games. Do you play a musical instrument or want to? Do you like listening to music? Perhaps you like a good chat?

Most auditory people speak quite slowly because they want to have time to choose the right words because the words are important just as it's important to them that the listener understands what they are saying.

You learn best by listening to the teacher rather than looking at what they've written on the board or asked you to read. You learn best by saying things over to yourself in your head. When you're revising, read out loud what you have in your notes and make use of any Internet sites that have sound.

Project work will suit you or having a revision buddy who can ask you questions rather than writing things down.

You could read your notes into the voice memo on your phone or use programmes like audacity to record MP3 files. Then you can transfer them to your phone so you can listen to them rather than read them. Check out podcasts and audiobooks to aid your learning as well as DVDs and YouTube videos.

For you, the sound of your ideal car will be what you notice and what people say about it. You probably want a car with a big noisy exhaust system and want a good sound system in the car. Whilst good sounds attract you, discordant sounds will annoy, so other people's music will be irritating as will noises of other people talking while you are trying to concentrate. You can manage that by using headphones to listen to your own music while you are revising.

C - Kinaesthetic

If you've answered more C then you are kinaesthetic. You are an active person and enjoy being physical and having physical contact with your friends and your family. You may have even been called 'hyperactive' when you were younger!

You talk about what you're doing or going to do and say things like 'let's get going' or 'what's happening?' Sitting still isn't easy and you soon get fidgety. Some kinaesthetic children walk around while they're working because this action helps them to focus. Homework is harder for you because you want to be active so break up your study time with some physical activity and do it in short bursts.

You want to actively participate in your learning. Project work and practical subjects will suit you such as Design technology, Food Technology, Science experiments and of course PE and sport. You also like any interactive computer learning. Make notes when you are listening and use highlighters to emphasise words or phrases because for you, active listening works best.

In addition to VAK we use filters to make sense of our world. So get your pen ready for some more quizzes.

BIG CHUNK/ SMALL CHUNK

Which are you?

When your teacher is telling you how to do something at school do you want to know all the detail and maybe ask him/her questions about it?

> Yes – I ask lots of questions
> No – I just have a go at doing it

Do you read the instructions on a new gadget or piece of software or do you work it out for yourself as you go along?

> Yes – I read the instructions
> No – I just work it out

When you read a book or magazine do you read it thoroughly or just skim read to get the general idea of the story?

> Yes – I read it thoroughly
> No – I just skim read

When you look at your friends' photos do you look at each one in detail or just look at the main subject?

> Yes – I would notice the detail
> No – I would just notice the main subject

In tests or exams do you always read the questions carefully and then go back and check you've answered every one?

> Yes – Of course
> No – I just get it over with and hope for the best

This is a preference for detail or concepts. If you are small chunk and answered mostly 'Yes' then you'll find it easy to do maths and science subjects where accuracy and thoroughness are important. You will be good at remembering dates and facts in other subjects like History or Geography but anything that is more analytical or with no definite right or wrong answer such as philosophy or religious studies may prove more challenging. If you prefer your information in small chunks, select a topic area within a subject to revise and put everything else away out of sight.

If you sometimes find yourself getting caught up in detail and feel overwhelmed, ask 'but what does this mean?' You may also find it helpful to write lists and tick things off as you do them.

If you mostly answered 'No' then you prefer 'big picture' thinking. You're good at getting an overall sense of what's needed and rarely get overwhelmed. However, you may sometimes make careless mistakes or forget things because you haven't checked your work before handing it in. Do you sometimes get the right answer but forget to explain how you got it?' The 'big chunker' is not fussed about accuracy so long as they understand the overall concept which may work in subjects that lend themselves to analytical thinking but won't always work if there is a definite right or wrong answer. You're great at coming up with ideas but when it comes to the organising you'll need to team up with someone 'small chunk'.

In teamwork and friendships the two work well together but you need to value what the other person's strength brings rather than being irritated by it. This is the same with most of these.

CHOICES/PROCESS

Do you like having choices?

Do you like to spend time deciding what to do?
    Yes
    No

Do you spend ages deciding what to pack for a sleepover?
    Yes
    No

Do you flick through the TV channels to look at all the choices before deciding what to watch?
    Yes
    No

When you go shopping do you enjoy looking in lots of different shops to see the choices?
    Yes
    No

When you go out to eat do you spend ages choosing from the menu?
    Yes
    No

If you mostly answered 'Yes' then you are 'choices' and if you answered 'No' you are 'process'. If you like choices, you'll introduce choices into every decision and spend time choosing when to do your homework or which topic to write an essay on, whether to have a glass of squash or juice, a sandwich or a toastie. This isn't going to get anything done! So if you are a 'choices' person you may just have to limit your choices and start!

'Process' children like lists of 'things to do' so they can tick them off. They prefer to be asked what they want rather than have to consider choices. If you don't want choices and are given them, it can be very confusing so you'll be tempted to just pick the first option you are given.

If you're sitting the 11+ then this is very relevant for you. If you like choices then you don't have a problem considering the multiple choice answers but if you don't like choices you will have to mentally tell yourself that you just want to look for the right answer and when you've found it, move on.

One is not better than the other. In some situations you might be 'choices' and other times 'process'.

TOWARDS/AWAY FROM

Here is another quiz for you.

When you have a meal do you think about what you want more of or what you want less of?
- A - More of
- B - Less of

At school do you look for who you want to hang out with or avoid who you don't want to be with?
- A - Look for friends
- B - Avoid who you don't like

Do you behave well to please your mum or teacher or because you don't want to get into trouble?
- A - Want to please
- B - Don't want to get in trouble

Do you tidy your room because you want to be able to find things or because you'll get told off if it's in a mess?
- A - Want to be able to find things
- B - Don't want it in a mess

Do you care about how you look or just want to avoid looking a mess?
- A – Want to look good
- B – Don't want to look a mess

Do you think about what you DO want or what you DON'T want? Do you think about what you want MORE of or what you want LESS of?

If you mostly answered 'A' then you are 'towards' and 'B' you are 'away from'. For example, a 'towards' child will think of what they want for supper and an 'away from' child will hope they don't get something they don't like. It doesn't matter which you are. If you are 'towards' you will want to get good marks at school and if you are 'away from' you want to avoid getting bad marks.

Both are OK. However, if you are 'away from' ask yourself sometimes 'What do I want?' or 'What do I want more of?' because you are more likely to get what you do want rather than not get what you don't want. We will be covering this in more detail in the chapter on motivation and goal setting as you can imagine. For now, just be aware of which you are and think about the word 'don't'.

If I say "Don't think about pink elephants!" what do you think about?

INTERNAL/EXTERNAL

How important are other people in your life?

☐ Do you ask your friends for recommendations before
   buying a new video game?
   Yes
   No

☐ Do you usually get the same brands as your friends?
   Yes
   No

☐ Do you think about what your friend wants before
   buying their birthday present?
   Yes
   No

☐ Do you tend to see the movies your friends are talking
   about?
   Yes
   No

☐ Are you quick to notice when one of your friends looks
   a bit sad?
   Yes
   No

If you answered mostly 'Yes' then you are externally
referenced and tend to be very influenced by other people
in your life; what your friends say and what they like and
don't like.

An internally referenced person will decide for themself. It can be very useful to be able to switch from external to internal referencing because this is a good way to protect yourself from bullying and peer group pressure. For example, if you want to please people and you want them to like you over and above what is important to you then you will find yourself agreeing to things that you don't want and you won't stand up for what you believe in.

Here's how to do it:
Imagine you can float out of your body and look at what is going on from the outside, like a webcam. What can that webcam see, hear and feel? Is what they are saying or doing what I want to be part of?

You can't be totally internally referenced because then you wouldn't care what <u>anyone</u> thought so you'd be very unpopular. The ideal is for you to ask yourself 'what do <u>I</u> think about this?', 'how does it fit with what <u>I</u> value?' As you do that, you check in with your internal referencing system. Practice switching between the two to give yourself flexibility and control.

MATCH/MISMATCH

Try this quiz!

When you meet someone new what do you notice?
- a) What you have in common
- b) How different you are

When you compare your homework with a classmate's do you notice?
- a) What you have written that is similar
- b) What is different

When you go to a party do you notice how…
- a) Similar you look to your friends
- b) How different you look

When you get your homework back do you notice…
- a) What you've got right
- b) What you got wrong

When you are chatting with your friends are you
- a) Usually agreeing
- b) Disagreeing

Clearly 'a' answers are matching and 'b' is mismatching. Matching can be verbal or non-verbal and ideally both in order to achieve maximum rapport. Matching body language is the first step in making friends and influencing people.

During puberty, children often find that they want to mismatch in order to be noticed or to be a bit independent. However, when you want to make friends it is better to match. This means looking/listening/doing (depending on your VAK) similar things so you have common ground to build on. In exactly the same way, when you make an important change in your life such as moving schools or moving house, look for what there is in common, points of similarity and what you like and agree with in order to make an easy and successful transition.

When you're negotiating with your parents; find something to agree about first e.g. "I agree it's important to get enough sleep" or "I agree it's important to get my homework done". Then add 'and' rather than 'but' because anything before a 'but' isn't heard. Then explain what you want and by matching you have more chance of a win/win negotiation.

Knowing how you process information helps you understand how you learn and how you communicate with others. When you know how you learn best you also know how to improve your grades and what revision techniques to use. Knowledge is power!

Make a note now about which you are.
VISUAL
AUDITORY ♪ ♫ = me
KINAESTHETIC

BIG CHUNK/SMALL CHUNK
CHOICES / PROCESS
INTERNAL/EXTERNAL REFERENCE
TOWARDS/ AWAY FROM ⟵
MATCH/MISMATCH

Now think about the other important people in your life. Do you get on better with people who are the same as you? What can you do now to get on better with those who are different?

CHAPTER 2: SO WHAT IS NLP THEN?

Let's break it down. NLP stands for Neuro Linguistic Programming.

Neuro is how we think. When you and your friends all go to the same movie you notice different things don't you? This is because you process your world slightly differently – we've just learnt about this in the last chapter. What you think is what you get as you'll find out as you read this workbook.

Linguistic is what we say and how we say it. We also have that inner voice which sometimes helps us but often hinders. The words we use will affect the outcome we get and those words are chosen by the thoughts we had.

Programming is what happens, the result and those habits we have of running the same patterns even when they don't get us what we want.

NLP was developed by Richard Bandler and John Grinder who were interested in what makes some people successful, popular, highly skilled etc. They did a study of these people from all walks of life; business, sport, music and found that they held certain beliefs that were unique to them. They then coded these beliefs into what they called NLP and found that anyone who applied this code would achieve this success. 'Success' can mean financial success but it can also be getting into the school sports teams, doing well in exams, being invited to a cool event, being popular at school, hanging out with the fit boy/girl and so on.

Here are the beliefs for you to apply in your own life. They may be new to you and different from what you believe right now. If the results you're getting now could be better then see what results you get with these beliefs.

It's easy to change a belief. Beliefs are not facts (e.g. 25 is the number after 24) nor are they values (e.g. it is important to be honest). They are what we hold to be true at this time e.g. belief that if you work hard you'll get a good mark. It's not a fact that you will. The value is 'working hard'. So try these beliefs out for yourself.

1) *If you always do what you've always done then you will always get what you've always got*

If what you are doing now isn't getting you what you want, you need to do something different. It's no good expecting other people to change because you don't have control over them but you do have control over your own behaviour. If you want a different result it's <u>you</u> who has to change.

Here's an example:

Joe was coming up to his GCSEs but he didn't have much hope that he'd get good grades. After all, every exam he'd ever taken at school he'd done badly in. "I don't understand it" he moaned "I read through my books and all my essays the week before, I look through everything."

He was just hoping that this time it would be different but it won't be because he's simply repeating the same unsuccessful pattern. What he needs to do is something different. He needs to think about what he does when he gets good results and copy that structure.

It takes Joe a while to remember exam successes but then someone reminds him that he used to get all his spellings right in Primary School. How did he do that? He racked his brain trying to remember. Of course, he'd written them out again and again! So Joe applied this structure, writing out his notes instead of just reading them. Guess what! He got great grades!

So here is a new way of thinking. Do something different. When you do something different you get a different result.

Think of a result you're getting that you want to change.

Write it down here.

I want to change.....buying.......virtual.....games+.....things.......I....feel.......like.....it's.....waesting.........my.......and.......my....parents.....money.

Now think about what you would like to happen instead. We call this your 'compelling outcome'? Write that down now.

What I want to happen is.... _to_ ...... _spend_ .... _money_ ... _wiserly_ ....

....

Be specific and get to the detail. What <u>exactly</u> do you want, from whom, when and in what way? Write this down here.

I want ...... _everyone_ ...... _to_ .... _understand_ . _that_ .... _i_ ... _know_ ... _I_ ...... _have_ _alota_ ... _stuff_ ...... _but_ ...... _I_ ... _earned_ ...... _it._ ......

The more specific you can be about what you want to happen, the easier it will be to decide how to change what you are currently doing in order to achieve it. You know sometimes even though we say we want a different result, there is something holding us back from getting it. There can be several things that get in the way but the main one is what you believe is possible, for you.

Do you find yourself saying "but I can't do…the dishwasher" or "I can't…be confident"?

These are 'limiting beliefs'.

Our beliefs stem from early childhood and how we were brought up, what you consider to be of value and important to you. They may also come from the culture you are from, the area or region and who you have grown up with.

If what you are doing is not working then look at the underlying belief behind this behaviour. An underlying belief is what you believe to be true about something so for example,

A 15 year old dancer told me that she doesn't get nervous when she goes on stage for her solo dances but she gets very nervous just before her group dances. Her belief is that she will let down the rest of her group.

Are you sure your underlying belief is sound? Could you be carrying forward into the present a belief that belongs in the past? Look back at the situation you have written about and list all the beliefs that affect your thinking. What beliefs do you have about what <u>should</u> happen in that situation?

I believe that...........

I believe that............

I believe that..............

Where have your beliefs come from?

Are they valid for you today?

Are they serving you well or making life more difficult?

Could you re-think a belief so that you could make another choice of behaviour?

Whenever you find yourself thinking 'I should do....' - change it to, 'I could do...' so that you give yourself permission to do something different.

Do your beliefs limit your choices of behaviour? Increase your options and change your behaviour to get the result you want.

Consider each option and how likely each one is to bring about the outcome you want.

This process requires that you step into the shoes of the other people involved in your situation rather than just look at it from your own perspective. This is an enormously powerful tool that you can learn now and apply throughout your life. When you find yourself saying 'I can't do.....' ask yourself instead, 'and what if I could?'

What difference would it make in your life if you <u>could</u> do the thing you believe you can't do? How about believing that you can do it, right now! Act as if you can, visualise that you can and you're already there. This is called 'acting as if'.

Another thing that can happen that stops us doing something different is that we get a 'pay off' for doing what we usually do. This 'payoff' can be getting attention or being thought 'cool' or being part of a gang.

Niki wants to be popular at school so she agrees with whatever is suggested even if it is stealing from local shops or smoking behind the bus shelter near school. She knows that if she gets caught, her parents would be angry and disappointed and she might be excluded from school but the payoff is more important to her.

So the question is how can she still be popular but without doing things she knows are wrong? She needs to do something different and that might mean making different friends. What would you suggest?

> worry about school first and chat to somepeople that look nice and mature.

To summarise then,

- Think about what you want
- If you're not getting it do something different

2) You have the resources to do whatever you want to do

A resource is a skill, something that you are good at. You have a huge number of skills but when you're good at something you don't always realise it until someone points it out because we tend to take our skills for granted. Yet each one can be used in a slightly different way in another context and this gives you even more skills and options. Here's an example.

Maybe you can do 'keepie uppies', or write funny poems,
sing in tune...................

What can you do really well, write it down here.

...............drumming.................................

Now what else does this mean you can do? Here are a
few ideas, tick all those that you can do as a result of that
one thing you've written down.

Concentrate ✓
Learn to do something
Stand on one leg
Practice until you get it right ✓
Show patience
Teach someone else how to do something ✓
Focus on one task ✓
Balance

Now add some of your own

Do you get the idea?

What we're saying is that one skill leads to another and another and so on. So if you're brilliant at concentrating on your Xbox game or PS game then that skill for concentrating can also be used at school or for doing your homework. Yes really!

If you can learn to do one thing then you can learn how to do anything when you transfer the strategy.

Let's write a list now of all your skills.

1. drumming
2. focusing
3. gaming
4. making music
5.
6.
7.
8.
9.
10

So if you are feeling low self-esteem, imagine that someone is watching you over the course of the day. What would they observe? What would they see you do?

What you do automatically or unconsciously is a skill that someone else observing would admire. Pretend you are someone who doesn't know you, observing all you do.

- Look at each thing you do over the course of the day and write down the skill you use to do that thing.
- What do you believe about doing this thing? How important is the way you do it? How well do you feel you do this thing?

The reason I do............... _music + gaming_ well

is because I believe......... _in reaching my goals_

The reason I do......... _my goals_ ......well

is because I believe........ _in my self_

The reason I do......... _gaming_ ......well

is because I believe....... _to have fun_

The reason I do......... _drumming_ ......well

is because I believe......... _to be happy_

Now list each thing you do well and give each one a score out of 10 for how important it is to you to do this thing well.

1. drumming   10

2. gaming   6

3. being happy   0

4. feeling bad   10

5. feeling guilty 10

Now look at each thing you do and ask yourself, 'What does that <u>also</u> mean I can do?'

Write that down in a list here. You may be surprised at how you can use a skill in many different parts of your life.

- When you are struggling

    o identify the skill you need

    o think about when and where you had that skill

    o ask yourself, what was the belief you had that enabled you to use that skill

    o accept that belief now in order to access the skill.

When we talk about taking on a belief in NLP we mean that we change our belief. This is a bit like changing the belief that you used to have in fairies or monsters.

A belief is something you hold to be true about the things you do and they change as you experience new situations and people. Do you have any of these beliefs?

What are your limiting beliefs? What are the things you think you 'can't' do? Write them here.

I can't....... *I can't get my phobias out of the way*

I can't....... *make friend*

I can't....... *do my homework done*

I can't...

I can't...

Think of a time when you didn't have that belief. You certainly weren't born with it!

What could you do then, what skills did you have then or in that situation that you need to have now?

Write them down here:

I went to go ape and one task was very scary, I was going to quit but did it.

You still have that skill; so use it to do whatever it is you want to do now. You <u>do</u> have all the resources you need. You can learn can't you? Whatever skill you need that you don't have, can be learnt. Read on!

3) *If someone else can do it you can too*

Do you find yourself looking at one of your friends and wishing you could do whatever they are doing? Would you like to add their skill to your list? Well you <u>can</u> you know!

The fact that you have noticed the skill means that you have the potential to do it too. We say 'if you spot it, you've got it!' It doesn't have to be a skill like juggling or scoring from the half way line, it could just be that this person has a skill of being able to listen attentively so that people want to talk to him/her or they're popular at school, get really good marks or always get picked for the teams. Maybe they're good at art or music? It could just be that they have a cute smile!

You can get this new skill and work on your existing ones by a process we call 'modelling' which is like copying. We are going to copy what they do because they do it so well and we'd like to be able to do it too. So how do we do it?

a) First you need to decide which skill you want.

It's easy to get distracted by the <u>whole</u> skill when actually what you may want is just a small part of it. So look carefully and try to identify which bit of the skill you need from your model (the model is the person who can do the thing you want to do). You might use several models because it usually takes a few goes to 'get it' and some people are just better than others at explaining how they do something and what their thinking is.

<u>Example</u>
I love hockey and want to be better at tackling but it is not the entire tackle from approaching the opposition to getting the ball off them that I wanted to copy. I can do the beginning and the end, it's the actual bit just after the contact that I wanted.

So break the skill into steps that you have observed and do a mental check to decide which you can do and which you'd like to improve on. Decide which bit you need and break it into small parts that you can practice.

Watch every part of the skill, the non-verbal cues such as body language and the verbal ones, the tone of voice, language patterns, volume and pace.

   b) Think about the belief your model must have in order to use that skill.

Do this by reflecting "If I were doing this, I would be thinking .... *about the good sides* ...."

Think hard about where you have the belief and visualise yourself in that situation where the belief is strong.

Even in mixed schools boys and girls feel awkward around each other; some more than others. If you find this aspect difficult then copy the pattern of someone who seems to find it easier. What do they do? What do you think they believe? Where do you have this belief yourself? Try it on for size.

c) Now practice the precise skill you have identified. You can do this on your own first and then practise on your friends.

Notice the results you get and keep practising until you get your desirable outcome. Then model other people and other skills. You can even practise by copying a character from your favourite soap, celebrity or sportsperson you like to watch. Take one aspect such as how they move their head or their arms and have a go yourself.

It's really important to be curious and wonder how it is that this person can do the thing you want to copy because if you use your own thinking (the thinking that can't do this skill) then you won't get it because it's the thinking behind it that is making the difference. New skills mean new thinking.

4) There is no failure only feedback

Let's face it. At one time or another we all feel a failure don't we? Things don't always go as we'd like and when that happens we get upset and feel we've failed. Sometimes we don't feel a failure ourselves but our teacher or parent tells us we've failed when they criticise us. Maybe the failure is in the form of bad marks, poor grades or an embarrassing school report. It could be playing badly in a match or losing a good friend.

But what if I tell you that there is no such thing as failure?

failure = feedback

What I mean here is that you <u>have</u> to fail in order to learn. Scientists endlessly carry out tests and eventually they find a cure or a solution but they don't consider all their tests to be failures do they? And nor should you.

When you kept falling over as a toddler trying to stand up and walk, you didn't give up did you? You hadn't failed. You simply hadn't got it right <u>yet</u>. You just keep trying, maybe tweaking this and that and eventually you get it right. That is called 'learning'.

What can we learn from what went wrong so that there is a good positive outcome?

Think about the last time you thought you'd failed. Write down what happened or what the situation was.

I was very homesick and I didn't want to go to the school

Now think of at least three things you learnt from that experience.

1......*that....im.......safe*..............

2.....*that........its......going.....to....be great*

3...*I......made....friends*........................

Go on, I bet there's a fourth!

4..*I.......get.......good......practise*......

How we choose to respond to feedback or criticism will be determined by what you think of yourself.

There is no <u>one</u> correct response.

When someone criticises you, remember that they are giving you feedback for you to learn from. How you learn is up to you but first check that what they are saying is reasonable because it may not be.

You may be being told off in class for something you did not do. There is learning in this e.g. be more careful next time who you sit next to! The feedback is simply someone's opinion at that moment and it may be incorrect. It may even be influenced by whether they were kept up last night by a crying baby, had a row with their wife, were just dumped on by the Head or had a flat tyre on the way in to school.

You have two choices when you get negative feedback. You can choose to accept it or reject it. Whatever you do, remember there is learning for you.

Accept it if you think they may have a fair point and take the opportunity to reword what you said or do something differently. By doing this you are using the feedback as a learning experience that will enable you to do something better next time.

If you decide that it is unreasonable then you can choose to ignore it or say that you don't agree with it.

Do you sometimes have to give feedback to others? Here's a really good way of doing it. It's called a feedback sandwich. Give yourself one now just to practise.

1. *What did I do well today?*

......making.......friends..............

2. *What would make it __even__ better next time?*

......being.......confident..............

3. *What was good overall?*

......I....had....a....good....time........

Feedback is all around us. It is in the way someone looks at you, what they say to you, how they respond to what you say to them. It is verbal of course but often also non-verbal and it can be quite obvious or slightly hidden.

Remember though that in the feedback is a present for you. There is a gift of learning. So next time you get a bad school report or a disappointing grade, ask yourself

"What is the learning here? What will I do differently next time?"

5) If you try, you won't succeed

OK own up! How often do you tell your mum you'll 'try and do this' or tell your teacher you'll 'try and do that'? Does it happen? No!

Why doesn't it happen?

Because in your head you know you won't actually do it, you'll just 'try' and do it.

We want to keep our options open really, don't we? We don't want to give a promise that we may not be able to keep and we don't want to let people down or appear rude by saying 'no'. So off we go to 'try' and do that thing, knowing that we don't have to do it, we just have to 'try' to do it.

Exercise

Put two cans of baked beans or something similar in front of you.

Tell yourself to 'try' and pick up one of them. Have a go.

Now tell yourself to just pick the other one up. Have a go.

Which seemed lighter?

Come on! You know they both weigh the same!

Do your teachers ask you to 'try your best'? If you're taking the 11+ do your parents say 'just try and do your best, that's all we ask' and yet you know perfectly well that they want you to pass.

Notice when you use this word then reword your sentence without the word 'try' so you will be more motivated. 'Try' presupposes you will find it difficult so you will give up on the exercise more quickly than if your expectation is that you can do it. There is built-in failure in the word 'try'. So if you are 'trying' to work hard, lose weight, pass your 11+ or your SATS ....

Just 'do it'!

6) *The map is not the territory*

How you view your world of school and home, your friends, hobbies and outside school interests is not how your parents view them is it? Each of us has a unique and slightly different view of things. How we see them will be based on our age, gender, how we've been brought up and the experiences we've had.

Example

My 11 year old son was listening to his IPod in the car going to school this morning. It sounded terrible to me. I said "Could you turn that down it sounds terrible" and he said "It sounds terrible to you because you can only hear the beat, I can hear the music". I thought this was a great metaphor for how parents and children perceive things differently.

To assume our own perceptions are the only correct ones would in NLP terms be called 'unecological'.

This is obvious when you consider how your parents see their world. Their map is very different from yours. In many ways their world is quite boring compared to yours. They have to work, earn money, pay bills and look after you. This will continue for the foreseeable future. However, they know that once you've finished your school-life ideally with good grades, the world is your oyster! They hope for such a good life for you and can see the bigger picture of what is in store for you. Their map for you is big. However, at this moment in time for you, your map looks very different and probably seems small, confined and restricted to what you have to do and what you are allowed to do.

Because your map is smaller and more intense, any changes have more impact, whether that is a change of teacher, moving schools, or your parents splitting up. You fear change because so much is still unknown to you and you have limited experience to reassure you that it will be OK. Whereas when adults encounter change they usually have something similar that they can draw on for reassurance and confidence.

If you have to make a significant change in your life either because you have made that choice or because it has been decided for you then remind yourself of other changes you have coped well with and take on the belief that you will be fine, just as you were last time.

The main change you will have to manage is moving to secondary school isn't it? How are you feeling about it at the moment? Write down what you are looking forward to first in the box below. This is what we call 'towards thinking'. I am looking forward to....first.....day...of year 7

What is going to be similar at your new school? This is called 'matching'. We tend to feel much more comfortable about change when we focus on what will be similar. Write these things in the box below.

Close your eyes and imagine you are at your new school right now.

What do you look like, what are you wearing?
What are you doing?
Who are you with?
What sounds can you hear?

When we project our thoughts into the future and imagine ourselves in the new situation this eases the passage of change for us.

Now close your eyes and think back for a moment to when you first started at your current school. You were a lot younger of course so you need to shrink yourself down to the size you were then in your head.

What do you look like, what are you wearing?

What are you doing?

Who are you with?

What sounds can you hear?

Now open your eyes and be aware that you have already been through a change in schools when you first arrived at this school. You got through it didn't you? You made friends and you had a great time. The same will be true for you at your secondary school because you already have the skills you need and the experience of having done it before.

Example

Even famous actors are nervous before a new play starts or before filming a new movie. They experience sweaty palms and butterflies in the stomach. They say it is a mixture of worries that things will go wrong and excitement about the things that will go right. When they start to experience the nerves they welcome them, knowing that this is what will insure they do a great performance.

Moving to secondary school is a bit like that isn't it? Remember the map is not the territory though. If you're worried about the move you can be pretty sure that your parents are even more worried as they see this as a huge step in your life and theirs. It is your choice whether you take that step with a big smile on your face and a positive attitude or whether you choose not to. You will have plenty more choices when you start secondary school so use this book to explore how to make positive choices that are best for you.

We've just been thinking about the move to secondary school but we may have other changes to cope with and not all of them are positive are they? As children you don't get much say in what happens to you and will have to do things you don't want to do and feel resentful about. You may also have to be stopped from doing things you <u>do</u> want to do and feel resentful about that too.

Again you have a choice. You can decide to feel really angry or you can look for the positive intention. Your best choice is to assume that your parents love you and that your teacher wants the best for you so step into their map and look at the situation from another angle.

Be curious about what their positive intention is. Imagine yourself in their shoes. If you were doing or saying this, what might be the positive reason? Perhaps this is their reason too?

Once you understand their positive intention you can negotiate for what you want by offering them another way for them to get this. This way you have a 'win win'.

For example, if your parents want you to do your homework or revise for some tests rather than go out, the positive intention is for you to do well. Perhaps you could agree to do an hour's work before you go out? What other options might there be to meet that positive intention with a behaviour you would find acceptable and that meets your objectives? It may be that you simply have to do something you don't want to do so be creative and find the 'up' side of it. There will be a positive angle if you look hard enough and if you are curious and creative.

This is a type of 'reframing' and it gives us another view of a situation where there will be some benefit from what at first glance seems a negative one.

How creative can you be? Be creative and find some good things about what you don't like doing.

This is a great skill because it gives us control over our emotions and environment. Being able to put a positive spin on unpleasant things will really help you through life.

We can't get on with everyone and you probably have kids in your class who you don't like much. Be creative, test your reframing skills and think of three things you like about them and three ways in which you are similar to them.

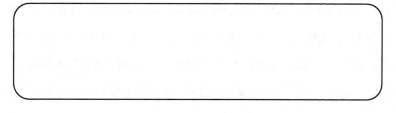

Boys and girls are different, yes really! Their map is different and sometimes a mystery. Apply the same process by being curious about their map and look for a win/win.

CHAPTER 3. I'M OK YOU'RE OK - CONFIDENCE

Remember in the last chapter you listed all the things you could do well and discovered that this meant that there were a whole load of other things you could also do well?

When we can do something well we usually feel confident for example, when we've practised or revised and know we've prepared as best we can. We feel confident when we're with people we like and who like us. Generally when we feel confident we feel calm and able to cope with whatever is required. That's a good feeling isn't it? Write down when you feel this good feeling of confidence.

when feeling like you know the topic really well and you know everything.

You may find that your confident feelings relate to your VAK. For example a visual person might feel especially confident when they know they look good. An auditory person may feel confident when they've played a piece well on the piano or sung well, spoken well. A kinaesthetic person will feel confident when they play a good match or do something really well.

Does this remind you of other confident times? Write down some more examples of when you feel confident.

when everyone started Jamming to my beat

Do you notice a pattern? Do you tend to feel confident in certain types of situation?

What we're going to do now is anchor them. An anchor is an association or link. When you go past a McDonalds and smell the burgers you probably think you're hungry and want to buy one. The smell is a trigger. This is a subconscious anchor because you did not intend to make the association. We are going to set up a conscious association so that we can use the trigger whenever we want to feel confident and have high self-esteem. You can use it on your first day at a new school or on a first date, when you have to give a talk to the class or do anything you're a bit nervous about.

Here's how we do anchoring.

Your anchor could be an image or a picture (if you are visual), a sound or piece of music (if you are auditory) or an action (if you are kinaesthetic).

Choose an anchor that you can use anywhere because it can be a bit embarrassing otherwise! Lots of people use this one by putting your thumb and first finger together.

People in business and sport use anchors when they want to access confidence, calm, energy or focus. You can have different anchors for different strengths.

<u>Step 1 – Establishing the anchor</u>

Close your eyes and think about when and where you feel calm and relaxed, strong and in control. Picture yourself there in that situation as if it is happening now.

What can you see? Give the scene colour and clarity. Turn up the brightness and focus on everything in your picture. What can you hear? Is there music? What are people saying?'

What are you doing? What is happening? Is it hot or cold? How do you feel?

When you really feel you are living the moment as if it were happening right now and feel as calm and confident as you could possibly be, fire the anchor. In other words, do the thing you have decided to do as your anchor. When the feeling starts to fade, remove the anchor.

Step 2 – Break state

Think of something else for a moment just to relieve the tension. If you are visual, look at something else. If you are auditory hum a tune and if you are kinaesthetic, walk about for a minute.

Step 3 – Fire it again

Repeat step 1 and again make the images, sounds and feelings very strong before you fire the anchor. Again remove it when it starts to fade.

Step 4 – Break state

Change your state for a minute – shake yourself or move about a bit.

Step 5 – Fire it again

Repeat the process. It will probably be quite quick by now.

Now you have your anchor, use it whenever you need that resource. You can establish different anchors for other resources.

The anchor is a metaphor; one thing representing something else. An anchor is very appropriate because when we feel lost, confused and overwhelmed it is helpful to put down an anchor to stabilize ourselves and find a calm place in our mind and body. We can rely on the anchor because it is heavy and solid and it won't let us down. From that calm place we can access our resources to move forward in what we're doing. We use anchoring to achieve a sense of control and resourcefulness in any situation.

Another reason to anchor is that sometimes we need to remind ourselves of good times to help us through more challenging times.

The sense of calm you get from anchoring can help you find that inner strength when and where you need it. You can anchor anywhere at any time and it takes seconds.

Example

Ellie was really nervous about taking the 11+ exams and her mother brought her to me to learn how to anchor so she would be calm for the exams. Ellie and I talked about when she was calm and she told me about her cat Pickles. Whenever she wanted to calm down she stroked Pickles. So I established an anchor with Ellie where she stroked her arm as if she was stroking Pickles. She would easily be able to do this in her exam without anyone thinking it was strange. She used her anchor and said she was calm the whole time.

Has this given you an idea for what you can use as an anchor? Write it down here because you'll be doing an anchoring exercise again later in the book so you might want to have a reminder.

A variation on anchoring which you might like to have a go at is the Circle of Excellence.

Here we imagine a circle drawn on the floor, large enough to stand in. You could use a belt to mark it out the first time you do it, to make it a bit easier.

Now close your eyes and think about a time when you felt really confident. It doesn't matter if it was a school thing, sport or social; you just need to capture that feeling of being calm, confident and able to cope with anything. We sometimes call that feeling 'resourceful' in NLP.

Notice as you think about this time how your body physiology changes. Look in the mirror. Are you standing taller with your back straight and shoulders down? Some people can quickly get their confident state just by getting themselves in the body shape that they associate with feeling confident. Can you do that?

Now when you are really 'into' that confident feeling, step into the circle and enjoy the feelings. This is your anchor, the step. When the feelings fade, step out and break state by giving yourself a little shake. Repeat this a few times thinking of different occasions when you felt confident.

The reason we've introduced anchoring and the circle of excellence in this chapter on confidence is to give you a choice. One may work better for you than another. You're probably already using anchors without realising it for example, when you wear a favourite piece of jewellery when you go out somewhere special or have a 'lucky band' for sport.

Be aware of when you feel confident and notice it. What you focus on is what you get more of, so use these confident occasions to add to your anchor to make it stronger. This is called 'chaining anchors'.

Also think of yourself as a confident person because if you label yourself as 'shy' or 'not very confident' that's what you'll be. This is why it's important to notice when you <u>are</u> what you want to be.

CHAPTER 4: I WANNA BE...............

You probably have no idea what you want to be when you leave school although most of us want to be 'rich and successful' if only we knew how! In the meantime we have more minor short term dreams that we call 'goals' or 'visions'. This is something you want to achieve, not a thing like a new video game or new mobile phone but something like:

- Making new friends

- Passing your exams

- Getting into a school football or netball team

- Moving up a set

What is your goal? Write it down here.

Check that your goal is:

1) POSITIVE

Write your goal down as what you <u>want</u>, not what you don't want or want 'less of'. It needs to be a 'towards goal'. If it isn't, rewrite it now as a positive goal.

Be aware that if your goal is to be slim, beautiful, healthy, fit, cool etc. that is fine and you will be when you set your mind to it but beware goals that are negative such as wanting to 'lose weight' or 'stop eating rubbish' because they won't happen. Think and focus on what you DO WANT.

How will you know when you have got your goal?

What sign or evidence do you need to show you have achieved your goal? Is it a mark, a level or a score? Is it some 'A's in your end of term report? Is it getting a part in the school play or a place in the sports team? How will you know you have reached your goal? You need to know so you can give yourself a pat on the back. This is also very important if you want to become slimmer. Set a sensible weight that will suit your frame and lifestyle and a reasonable time frame so that your body can adjust to the changes.

I will know I've got my goal when I ....
....
....

2) What and who do you need to help you?

Ask your parents or your teachers and friends to help you but if your goal relies on someone else doing something then it won't work. For example, if your goal is to win a race or come top of the class then it relies on other people doing less well than you. You can't control this so it is not a good goal. Instead set a goal that you can control.

What skills do you have that will help you achieve your goal? Write them down here.

3) What will be good about getting your goal?

Think about what benefits there will be to achieving your goal and what else you will be able to do once you have achieved it.

4) How will you cope with the negative consequences of achieving your goal?

Yes believe it or not, there can be negative consequences. Will you be called a 'geek' if you get good marks? Will your friends bitch about you when you're better looking than they are? Will you miss hanging out with your friends at break if you have to attend team practices? Think about how you can achieve your goal without negative consequences.

Let's have a quick look at why some people don't achieve their goals.

a) They define themselves according to what other people say about them e.g. "he'll never make the first team" or "she's so shy." You have the choice to be what you want to be and go for the goals that matter to you.

b) They didn't achieve this goal in the past so why will they succeed now? There is no such thing as failure, only feedback. Learn from your mistakes and move on.

c) They think they're unlucky. This is just silly; you make your own luck. Reframe and be positive and focused.
d) They say they are just being realistic about their chances. Are these other people's perceptions of reality? What is your perception?
e) If they can't be perfect or be the best then they don't want it at all. It is not possible to be perfect. Get as close to it as you can because that is good enough. Model the person who is best and you will get there.

A good way to find the resource you need for a challenging situation is to use the Time Line. This is an imaginary line along the floor that represents time. Imagine that at one end is the time when you were a baby and the other end is when you will be old, 30 say.

After you've done it once you'll find all sorts of occasions to use a time line. When you get to the stage when you have to choose your options for GCSEs and A levels it can be so hard to know which ones will be the most useful in your career when you don't even know what you want to do yet.

The Time Line is great for getting things into perspective when you feel a bit lost and lacking direction or if you have a big change coming up such as moving to secondary school, your parents splitting up or having a new family arrangement.

When you experience grief or loss, whether that is for a person or a part of your life such as leaving your Primary School, you can travel back along the time line, identify which skills you need from your old life, anchor them and bring them into the present as you move forward to Secondary School.

Once you've done the Time Line a few times it will be in your head and you can conjure up the image and the steps without moving. This can be useful in situations when you can't actually move physically, in class for instance.

We can combine the Time Line with anchoring by firing our anchor at significant points along the line as triggers for change and to help us access a feeling of confidence in the future as we mentally time travel. This is particularly useful for grief.

Step 1- Associate into it

So you have this imaginary line along the floor representing your life. Stand at the point representing today, the present. What do you see in your life? What images are there? Who do you see? If you are visual, give this colour, tone and form like a movie.

What do you hear? Who can you hear? Is there music? What sounds do you hear? If you are auditory make these into a band.

What do you feel? Are you warm or cold? Who is touching you? What are you doing? If you are kinaesthetic really move with the feeling.

Step 2 – Move to where you will have achieved your goal

This move will take you to a point on the line when you will feel happier, have achieved what you desire or have reached some significant point on your life's journey. Associate into this point as you did in Step.

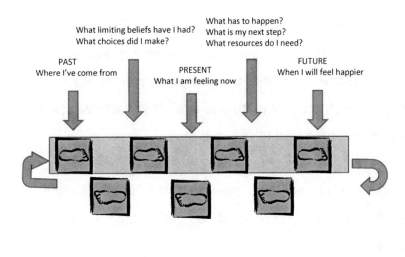

Step 3 – Move back to the present

In order to get to the desired point, things have to happen so what are the steps along the way to your goal? Walk through them one at a time, associating into each one.

Step 4 – Step back in time

Sometimes it can be helpful to step back along the time line if you find yourself saying 'I can't' or feel uncomfortable about something. By travelling back in time we can discover where these limiting beliefs came from and revisit them in terms of whether they serve us now. Travelling back in time we can go to the point when we felt brave or had confidence, when we could negotiate or make friends easily.

Associate into those times in the past, anchor the skill and travel forward again back to the present and take them with you into your future.

Goal setting can also be used in small everyday situations as well as these bigger changes. Constantly ask yourself what you want from each interaction during the day. What do you want to get from this lesson, this conversation, this match and imagine yourself achieving it. This is 'acting as if' and will give you a good chance of achieving what you want. After all, if you can't even imagine yourself achieving this thing, how would you recognise when you achieve it?

CHAPTER 5: EMOTIONAL UPS AND DOWNS

Do you remember in Chapter 2 we learnt how to reframe something by putting a positive spin on it and seeing it from another angle? This is what we need to do here.

You know how one day someone will say something to you and you're not bothered by it? Then the next day someone will say the same thing but this time it really winds you up? The problem is not what was said or who said it but it's all about YOU. How you choose to respond is the difference.

Let's call the outside force or the event 'pressure'. Most of the time we can cope with pressure and we just get on with things. In fact a bit of pressure can be fun and exciting and it can even bring out the best in us.

In fact, most of us work best under pressure. When time's short and deadlines loom, many people find they can be more charged up, more focussed and produce better work than when they sit at the computer playing with their phone. How do you work best? Do you like to get work done in plenty of time so you can relax or are you better under pressure? How much pressure is just right and when is it too much? Can you recognise the tipping point when the pressure is no longer productive?

So the question for us is this....how can we manage our mood so that we can take the positive aspects of pressure and minimise the negative consequences.

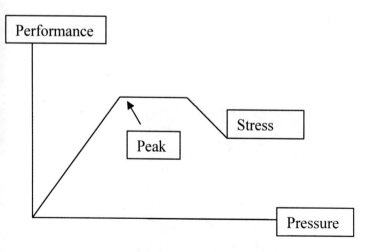

This graph shows that for most of us, performance improves as the pressure increases. During that build up you are maximising the positive force of the pressure and using it to produce results – performance. You are managing the stress and functioning effectively.

However, there comes a point when it all goes pear-shaped and we can't take any more. We haven't picked up our body's signals to eat, rest, take a break or exercise and now performance falls away after levelling off for a bit. There is a limit to how much pressure we can take.

The key to handling stress is to be aware of when you are no longer managing the pressure effectively. So what are the signs of stress?

1. If you can't sleep.

If you're having trouble sleeping at night that is a sure sign of stress. You need your sleep so that your body can function properly and recover ready for the next day. It's called 'beauty sleep' for a reason! We all need different amounts of sleep but we do all need to switch off completely and relax for at least 9 hours at your age. That doesn't mean texting your friends during the night!

2. If you're getting ill all the time.

If you seem to be constantly catching colds and bugs, this is your immune system not being able to protect you because you're run down and stressed.

3. If you're getting irritable and snappy with your mates and your family.

4. If you can't concentrate.

5. If you just can't step back, prioritise and make good
    decisions.

This could include getting caught up with the trouble
makers at school or in your street, not preparing for
important tests or arguing with your teachers and parents.

If you are experiencing any of these signs or several of
them then you are not managing your state and are
already on the downward phase of the graph. So how do
we avoid this happening in the first place and what can
you do about it right now? The first stage is a 'wind down'.

1. Accept the situation and take action.

2. Express how you feel by talking about it, writing, playing music, whatever works for you to release the emotional energy.

3. Then release the physical energy through exercise, run, walk, jog, play a sport and get that oxygen flowing through to your brain.

4. Now ground yourself by doing something special for yourself such as seeing a friend or watching something funny on TV, play music from your favourite band.

Then you need to wind up.

1. Think about what you want. What's important to you right now?

2. Set new goals and take control of them.

3. Take the first step towards the goal.

Another word for mood is 'state' and before we start thinking about how to control it, we need to know what your normal state is.

How are you when you are happy? Draw a picture below.

How would I be able to tell if you were happy? What would I notice about you? What would I notice about how you look, how you talk, what you say and what you do?

Now, draw a picture of you when you are sad, angry or in a bad mood.

How would I be able to tell if you were sad or angry? What would I notice about you? What would I notice about how you look, how you talk, what you say and what you do?

Now you know what to look out for when you are in different moods so let's SWISH the bad stuff away. Here's a really good way to do this.

Think about what happens just before you get into a bad mood. This is called 'the trigger'. It's like a gun; we pull the trigger in our head and 'bang' our mood changes. What we need to do is change our reaction to the trigger.

Is your trigger something you see (if you are visual) something someone says (if you are auditory) or something you feel (if you are kinaesthetic)?

Write down what happens <u>just before</u> you feel bad or angry or sad.

The trigger for me is.....................

Then what happens? Write it down here.

1) Make a picture in your head of what happens when you feel really bad and imagine it like a picture on the screen as if it's a movie at the cinema.

2) Now think of what you would like to happen <u>instead</u> next time that trigger goes off in your head. Write it down in the box below.

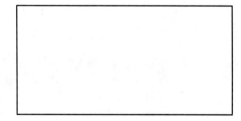

3) Make a picture in your head of this now and in your mind put it in the bottom left hand corner of the screen with your bad image in it.

4) Like this.

5) Now say out loud 'SWISH'. It sometimes helps to
   make a movement like swatting a fly away from
   your face. Then make the good image in the corner
   switch with the bad image in the middle like this.

You will need to practice it a few times and then you can use it every time you see, hear or feel that trigger in your head.

Now think about when you could use this technique and write your ideas in the box below.

Remember to use your anchor as well. You know how to anchor so establish an anchor for feeling calm and in control and use that when you feel that you are about to get angry or sad.

CHAPTER 6: MIND AND BODY R 1

Yes your mind and body are connected. You only have to look at yourself in the mirror and think really sad thoughts and you'll see how your body posture changes, how your face droops and how your body quickly reflects your thoughts. Now try it with happy thoughts – you look quite different don't you? If you're a sporty person you'll know how what goes on in your head affects whether you play well or badly.

Your body is changing daily through puberty and some of the changes you'll like, others you won't. You're filling out into a more adult shape and look less like a child. It's really important to love these changes and welcome them. Here in this chapter you'll find some ways you can use NLP tools and techniques to help you cope with the changes.

First be aware that no-one is happy with their body the way it is but when you focus on the bits you don't like then that is <u>all</u> that you'll see. Instead focus on all the good bits. Which bits of your body are you OK about? Write a little note about each on the illustration below.

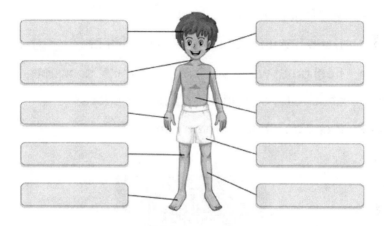

Do you realise that by focusing on what you're happy with; you'll feel happier about your whole body? You can focus on these bits by emphasising them in what clothes you choose, how you move and by giving them extra attention.

Maybe there will be parts of your body that you'd like to change. Lots of us want to be slimmer. You probably can't choose what your mum puts in the shopping trolley but you can choose what you eat during the day and you can increase your exercise.

You <u>know</u> what is fattening and what is healthy don't you?

A fairly easy way to a healthy diet and a better shape is to

- Eat fruit or nuts between meals
- Eat a breakfast, lunch, tea and dinner
- Feel great when you say 'no thanks' to sweets, chocolate, soft drinks, chips and crisps
- Exercise whenever you can

Instead of focusing on what you can't eat, focus on what you <u>can</u> eat. As a general guide, eat fresh food that hasn't been processed so eat fresh meat, fish and dairy, veg, fruit and water. You don't need anyone to tell you that if you eat fast foods you'll get fat.

Lots of children your age worry about their weight and the trouble is that the more you worry the worse it gets. Dieting will make you fat, especially fast faddy diets because your body will think it's being starved and will hold onto whatever fat you have.

A really good way to improve your appearance is by 'modelling' which is the NLP word for copying. We had a go at this earlier in the book. Here's a reminder.

Think of someone you know who has the body you'd like. It needs to be someone you know well as you're going to have to observe them and ask questions.

Observe

- How do they eat – fast or slowly? Pace them.
- Do they eat a lot at a time or a little? Match them.
- Do they snack or just eat at mealtimes?
- What food do they eat?
- How much exercise do they do and how much energy do they put into it?
- Are they quite active or do they sit around a lot?
- What do they drink?

Ask them

- What do you think just before you eat?
- How do you decide what to eat?
- How do you know when to stop eating?
- What are your favourite foods?
- How important is exercise to you?

If you can, copy what they eat and how they exercise because when you do what a slim person does and think the way a slim person thinks then you have more chance of looking how they look.

What beliefs do you have about food that could be limiting your ability to be slim? Do you feel you have to eat when you feel like it rather than when you are hungry? Do you drink sweet sugary soft drinks for energy because you're tired? Do you think you have no time for a run or a fast walk? Do you make choices that are making you fat? In the box over the page, write what you could do differently to get the body you want.

Also, when you keep your body clean, healthy and smelling fresh, people will be drawn to you and want to be close to you. During puberty cleanliness is particularly important so you may want to use deodorant and antiperspirant now if you've noticed that you are starting to smell under your arms during the day or after PE.

Get to know and love your body even the bits you'd prefer were different because just as you respond to positive attention so does your body. The more you attend to its needs by eating healthily and exercising, the more it will look good. If you ignore its needs, feed it rubbish and lie in front of the TV on the sofa it will soon look neglected.

You can use the mind / body connection to improve your sport and exercise. Think about how you look when you're performing well, running well doing your best physically. Watch how your body changes as your thinking changes. 'Act as if' you're the best footballer, hockey player or runner. Remember to use anchoring to anchor energy and commitment.

Remember the outcome depends on the thinking first followed by the behaviour. If you want a different result you need to change the thinking. At the beginning of the book we looked at the belief 'if you always do what you've always done, you will always get what you've always got.' Instead of blaming your lifestyle, parents, genes etc. take responsibility for your body and how it looks and behaves by changing the way you think about it.

CHAPTER 7. RELATIONSHIPS

As you move from being a child to being a teenager you will be seeking relationships rather than just having friends. Instead of being friends with everyone in the class as you were as a child, you will have a smaller group of friends with whom you feel close. You will also start having boyfriends and girlfriends so how can we make sure that these relationships are successful and give us what we need?

- Know who you are (Chapter 1) and be curious about who other people are. We do not all process our world in the same way but focus on matching with others and find similarities in order to build rapport and be popular.
- Like who you are (Chapter 3) by recognising what you do well and how you can learn from others to be even better.

- Set compelling outcomes (Chapter 4) for what you want in life; make them positive specific goals that are within your control.
- Take control of your 'state' (Chapter 5) by recognising when you are stressed and take action.
- Learn from setbacks and find a different strategy that works better and gives you the outcome you want.

Relationship work best when we avoid generalisations, distortions and deletions.

a) Generalisations

These are when we complain that someone 'always' does or says something or 'never' does something. For example; "my mum never listens", "my French teacher always gives me a low mark".

Generalisations are hardly ever true so they don't have much effect. In fact it's when you think of the exceptions that you learn something revealing. When was it not true? When <u>did</u> you get a good mark, what was different about what you did? Do the same again and test this out.

b) Deletions

This is being vague and missing out the detail so that what we say doesn't really make any sense. For example, "that's rubbish" – rubbish how, in what way, which bit of it, according to whom? You need some detail.

c) Distortions

Sometimes we make assumptions about what our friends, parents or teachers are doing and why they are doing it. We might say, 'you're deliberately annoying me' or 'you're making me cross'. They aren't. No-one can make you anything, it's your choice how you choose to react and respond.

What is really happening is that we are choosing to be cross or annoyed so we should tell them this instead and focus on the behaviour.

Be aware that drink and drugs create distortions and they mess with your head. At the time, we think they make us happy and fun to be with but this is the distortion. Being happy is your choice – nothing makes you happy.

Anything that affects your brain, limits your judgement and as a result, your choices.

Whatever your friends say; check in with your own values. This is being internally referenced (Chapter 1).Trust your gut instincts to make your own judgements. Ask yourself 'And what do I think?'

Mind reading is risky because we can't possibly know what is going on in someone's head, however well we think we know them. It's best to check it out.

Here's another interesting bit of background. Virginia Satir, whose work Bandler and Grinder (the founders of NLP) studied, explains that there are different behaviour types:

a) Blamer – aggressive, doesn't take responsibility for outcomes and typically says 'it's your fault'. You can get into this type by pointing your finger and saying things like "You should……." "You always………." "You never". Blamers tend to dominate and mismatch. They are bullies and want to dominate and intimidate you.

b) Placater – takes the blame for everything to keep the peace. Says 'yes' when they mean 'no'. Get into this type by lifting your chin up and your palms up with a "what did I do?" attitude. Placaters want to be liked and avoid confrontation and will be picked on by the Blamers. If you find yourself in this Blamer/Placater situation in your relationship you need to do something about it.

If you are the blamer – OK so now you know, that's a good start. Here are some questions for you.

What is your compelling outcome?

………………………………………………………………………………..

What is the benefit you get from this behaviour?

………………………………………………………………………………

How else could you get this benefit without the behaviour?

………………………………………………………………………………

Test it out!

The TOTE is a way of testing new behaviour.

Test – try it out

Operate - does it work?

If yes – exit

If no – go back and try another approach

If you are the placater then go back to Chapter 1 and remind yourself about internal /external referencing. Are you externally referenced? You need to practice being more internally referenced and checking in with yourself before responding in placater mode. What do YOU think? What do YOU want to do? Is this really YOUR responsibility? You are distorting the situation (see earlier 'distortion'. You may think that this is the best way to get people to like you but they do not respect you and it invites others to adopt the 'blamer' mode and you become the victim. Is this what YOU want?

Here are some questions for you.

What is your compelling outcome?

....

What is the benefit you get from this?

....

How else could you get this benefit without the behaviour?

....

c) Computer – weighs everything up and takes a view but doesn't get emotionally involved.

'Computers' use deletions in order to avoid getting involved and sound reasonable, calm and cool but disconnected. They are likely to quote facts and figures and avoid expressing their own opinion. Whilst it can be useful to sometimes disassociate in order to be able to take the emotion out of a situation, on a regular basis it can distance you from connecting and making friends.

d) Distracter – does anything for a laugh to avoid having to engage in the relationship.

These are the attention seekers at school who will do anything for a laugh, constantly change topic, make a joke out of any situation and tend to be unpredictable. They can be amusing for a while and entertaining but this mode needs to be controlled as it isn't always appropriate or advantageous. If you are a distracter just be aware of it and make a choice as to whether this is a good mode for the situation or relationship you want.

Like the computer above, it is another way of disconnecting and whilst amusing in the short term won't help you make long term friends.

e) Leveller – in touch with own emotions (internally referenced) and able to take on board other people's , grounded and open

This is a balanced mode where you have high self-esteem, can express your opinions in a reasonable way without causing offence and take on board those of others. You are after a win/win in relationships.

Let's see what all this means. Have you recognised yourself in any of these descriptions? So who are you in the relationships you have?

Who are you in your family? ……………………………

Who are you at school?……………………………………

Who are you with your friends? ………………………

The reason these Satir categories have been included here is to show how by recognising them and practising them you have access to a choice of behaviours depending on the situation. You may find that you tend to use a few of them or even mainly one of them but by using all of them you have a wider choice of behaviour.

For example if you have to make an important decision maybe in a group exercise or project, the 'distracter' role is not helpful and you might want to step into the 'leveller' to consider the options and move forward. However, if you are in the middle of a heated discussion the 'distracter' role may ease the situation and relax the tension. The 'placater' role is useful for calming down a situation and the 'blamer' is good when you want to be assertive if someone is being a bully. You could use the 'computer' when you need to keep your emotions under control during an exam.

This workbook has been all about choices. I hope it has introduced you to the wide range you have access to and shown you how by stopping and considering these choices rather than jumping into a situation you will have greater success in all your relationships.

NOTES TO MYSELF

Top 10 Tips 4 Happy Tweens

1) Focus on what you have, who you are and what is important to you rather than what others expect of you.

2) Check in with your own beliefs and values rather than comparing yourself to others.

3) We all make a mistake, that's how we learn. There is no failure, only feedback.

4) Notice what you have in common with others and be curious about differences, that's how to make friends.

5) In new situations and new places look for similarities to what is familiar.

6) Set compelling outcomes for what you want and build strategies for achieving them based on what you do well

7) You are communicating before you even open your mouth so make sure how you look communicates what you intend

8) Test Operate Test Exit - test new behaviour to check you get the result you want, if it doesn't keep testing until you do, then exit

9) You already have all the resources you need you just might need to track them down and transfer them

10) Everyone you meet has the potential to pass on a skill, be curious and be prepared to model the skill.

ALSO BY JUDY BARTKOWIAK

Teach Yourself: Be a happier parent with NLP
Teach Yourself: NLP Workbook
Teach Yourself: Self Esteem Workbook
Teach Yourself: Market Research in a Week
Secrets of Success in Brand Licensing

Engaging NLP series of workbooks
- For parents
- For children
- For tweens
- For teens
- For new mums
- For teachers
- For back to work/starting a business
- For health and fitness
- For sport
- For your relationship

JUDYBEE

Queens of Africa series
- Queen Amina of Zaria
- Queen Esther
- Madam Tinubu
- Queen Moremi
- Queen Idia
- Queen Makeda
- Learn Confidence

Zoo Crew play ball
What if sheep could fly?
What if hens were huge?
Danny goes to London

Buy my books
http://www.nlpandkidsbooks.com